Flea

Karen Hartley,
Chris Macro
and Philip Taylor

HEINEMANN
LIBRARY

For more information about Heinemann Library books, or to order, please telephone +44 (0)1865 888066, or send a fax to +44 (0)1865 314091. You can visit our web site at www.heinemann.co.uk

First published in Great Britain by Heinemann Library,
Halley Court, Jordan Hill, Oxford OX2 8EJ
a division of Reed Educational and Professional Publishing Ltd.
Heinemann is a registered trademark of Reed Educational & Professional Publishing Ltd.

OXFORD MELBOURNE AUCKLAND
JOHANNESBURG BLANTYRE GABORONE
IBADAN PORTSMOUTH (NH) USA CHICAGO

Designed by Ron Kamen
Illustrated by Alan Fraser at Pennant Illustration
Originated by Ambassador Litho Ltd.
Printed in China by South China Printing Co. Ltd.

04 03 02 01 00
10 9 8 7 6 5 4 3 2 1

ISBN 0 431 01705 0

British Library Cataloguing in Publication Data

Hartley, Karen
  Flea. – (Bug books)
  1. Fleas – Juvenile literature
  I. Title   II. Macro, Chris   III. Taylor, Philip
  595.7'75

Acknowledgements

The Publishers would like to thank the following for permission to reproduce photographs:

Ardea London: Bob Gibbons p.8, p.12, Francois Gohier p.28, John Clegg p.15, John Mason p.10, p.11, p.13, M Watson p.16, Stefan Meyers p.23; Bruce Coleman: Hans Reinhard p.25, Kim Taylor p.6; Bubbles: Jacqui Farrow p.17; FLPA: Silvestris p.5; Heather Angel p.26; Nature Photographers Ltd: NA Callow p.20; NHPA: Stephen Dalton p.27; Oxford Scientific Films: Alastair MacEwen p.4, GI Bernard p.24, London Scientific Films p.22; Planet Earth Pictures: Paulo De Oliveira p.29; Science Photo Library: Eye of Science p.7, JC Revy p.9, KH Kjeldsen p.14; Tony Stone: David Tipling p.19, NHMPL p.21, Wayne R Bilenduke p.18.

Cover photograph reproduced with permission of Peter Parks/Oxford Scientific Films.

Every effort has been made to contact copyright holders of any material reproduced in this book. Any omissions will be rectified in subsequent printings if notice is given to the Publisher.

Contents

Any words appearing in the text in bold, **like this**, are explained in the Glossary.

What are fleas?

Fleas are **insects**. There are about 2000 different kinds of flea in the world.

Fleas are called **parasites** because they live on other animals. Fleas only live on animals which are warm-blooded, like cats, dogs, sheep and even humans.

What do fleas look like?

Fleas have flat bodies which are shiny and hard. They have lots of sharp spines to stop them sliding off animals' hair. Fleas are usually brown.

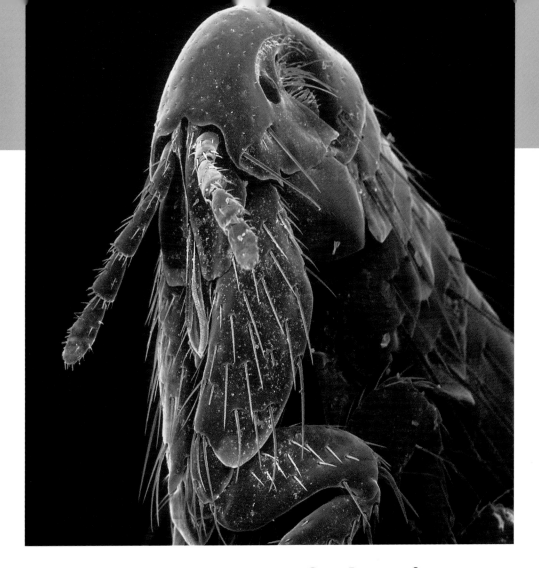

Fleas have two short **feelers** for smelling and feeling. Most fleas have large eyes but they only see shapes and know when it is light or dark.

How big are fleas?

Fleas that live on cats and dogs are smaller than the head of a pin. A flea that lives on a mole is the biggest kind and can be six millimetres long.

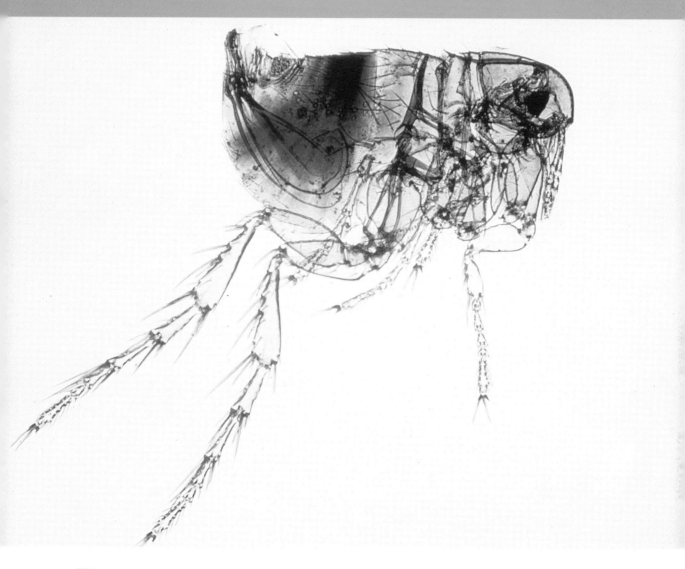

Fleas that live on people are bigger
than cat and dog fleas but they are still
very tiny. They are a bit bigger than the
head of a pin.

How are fleas born?

Female fleas lay hundreds of white eggs. Cat fleas can lay 25 eggs a day for three to four weeks. The eggs **hatch** after about five days.

When the **larvae** hatch they are long
and pale. They do not have eyes or legs
but have tiny hairs on their bodies to
help them wriggle about.

How do fleas grow?

Flea **larvae** eat dust and hairs in the **host** animal's sleeping place. They also need to feed on blood which **adult** fleas pass on in their **droppings**.

As it grows the larva **moults** twice. After two or three weeks the larva makes a **cocoon**. It is now called a **pupa**. The adult flea leaves the cocoon after about one or two weeks.

What do fleas eat?

A flea's mouth has a sharp, thin tube to stick into the **host** animal's skin and suck its blood. When fleas finish eating they usually drop off the animal but some stay on.

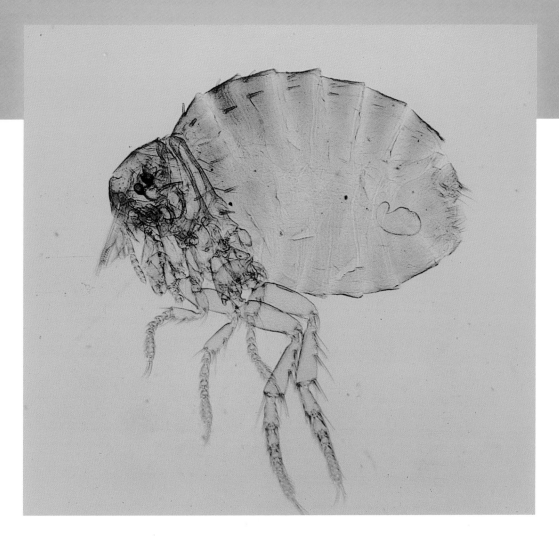

Jigger fleas bury themselves under the animal's skin and suck blood all the time. Jigger fleas can even bury themselves under people's skin!

Which animals attack fleas?

Flea **larvae** are fierce **predators** and they will kill and eat **adult** fleas that are weak. **Host** animals try to get rid of fleas by scratching themselves.

Fleas are pests so people kill them with special powders. When people **vacuum** their carpets they suck up the eggs and larvae.

Where do fleas live?

Most fleas live in countries where it is not too hot and not too cold. Some fleas can live in very cold places like the Arctic and the Antarctic.

Some fleas can live on people but most live on animals like cats, dogs, badgers and moles. Some fleas live on birds. Fleas live where animals sleep.

How do fleas move?

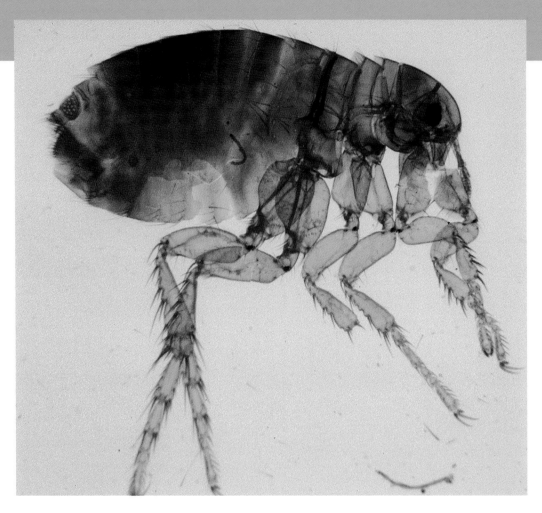

Fleas have three parts which make up their bodies. Each part has one pair of legs. Tiny claws on the legs cling to the animal's fur and hair.

Fleas do not have wings so they jump onto the **host** animal. Their back legs are very strong. Some fleas can jump as high as a 30 centimetre ruler!

How long do fleas live?

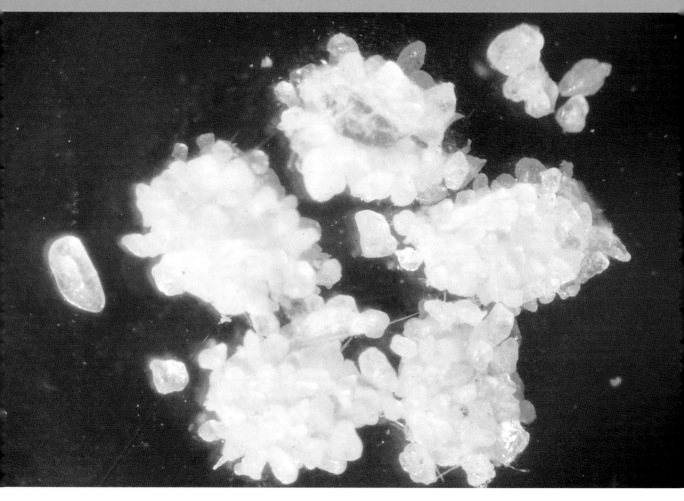

If it is cold fleas can stay in the **cocoon** for much longer than one or two weeks. When a flea does come out of its cocoon it will live for about six months.

Most fleas can live on different animals but some live on one kind. Rabbit fleas can only feed on rabbit blood, so if there are no **host** rabbits the fleas die.

What do fleas do?

When fleas suck blood they put **saliva** into the bite. The saliva is special because it keeps the blood flowing while the flea is sucking. It makes it itch afterwards.

If a flea sucks blood from an animal which is ill it makes the next animal it bites ill too. This cat is wearing a special collar which stops fleas biting it.

How are fleas special?

Fleas can live without food for a long time. If the **host** animal dies or leaves its sleeping place they have time to look for another host.

If there is no host animal when the fleas are ready to leave the **cocoon** they stay inside and wait. When an animal comes near, the fleas feel the movement or its body heat and jump on!

Thinking about fleas

Dinosaurs lived a very long time ago. They had thick, tough skin and no fur. Fleas did not live on the dinosaurs. Can you think why?

Fleas are able to jump very high and somersault over and over in mid-air. Can you remember how their long, strong legs help them to jump high?

Bug map

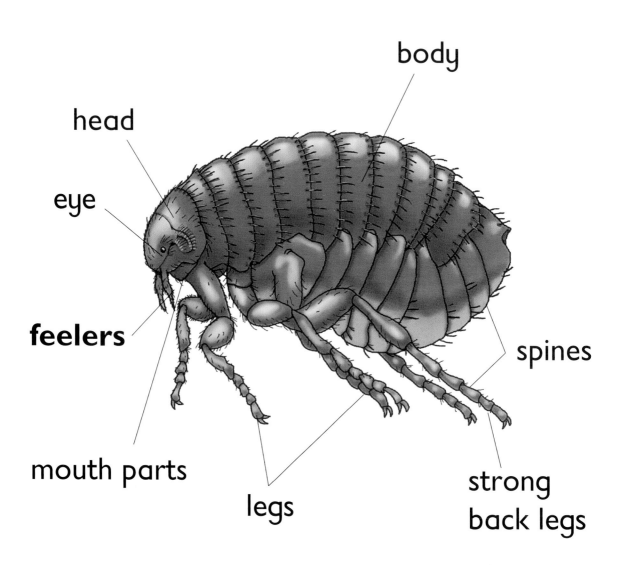

body

head

eye

feelers

mouth parts

legs

spines

strong
back legs

Glossary

adult   grown up

cocoon   a silky bag that the larva makes around itself

droppings   the body waste from an animal

feelers   thin tubes that stick out from the head of an insect. They may be used to smell, feel or hear.

female   a girl

hatch   come out of the egg

host   the animal on which the flea feeds

insects   small animals with six legs

larva   (more than one = larvae) the baby insects that hatch from eggs

moult   when the larva grows too big for its skin it grows a new one and wriggles out of the old skin

parasites   animals which live on other animals

predator   anything that hunts another animal

pupa   (more than one = pupae) the larva makes a case around itself before it turns into an adult

saliva   spit from the mouth

vacuum   a machine that sucks up dirt

Index